HORSES and PONIES

by
Robert Owen

HAMLYN

London·New York·Sydney·Toronto

For
D, F and A

Other books by the same author
My Learn to Ride Book
Successful Riding and Jumping
With John Bullock
The Young Rider
Buying and Keeping a Horse or Pony
Caring for a Horse or Pony
Riding and Schooling
About Jumping
The Horse and Pony Gift Book

Artists

Julie Chandler
T. Crosby-Smith
Gary Rees
Peter Swann-Brown
Tudor Art

Published by the Hamlyn Publishing Group Limited
London, New York, Sydney, Toronto
Astronaut House, Feltham, Middlesex, England
A Grisewood and Dempsey Book
Produced for the publisher
© Text Robert Owen 1978
© Grisewood and Dempsey Ltd 1978
Elsley House 24/30 Great Titchfield Street London W1
ISBN 0 600 34569 6
Printed and bound by Vallardi, Milan, Italy

Contents

Far left: Cleaning tack.
Top left: Riding side-saddle.
Bottom left: Two hardy little Icelandic ponies.
Above: A cream coloured mare and foal.
Below: The pleasure of pony trekking.

Acknowledgements

Cover: Equestrian (Press and General) Services Ltd;
Endpapers: Zefa
Title page: Zefa;
British Tourist Authority: 7 *bottom*, 48 *bottom left*, 56-57 *top and bottom*, 58 *top*, 59 *top*;
Equestrian (Press and General) Services Ltd: 6 *left*, 20 *bottom*, 22, 23 *bottom*, 24, 25 *top*, 26, 27, 28 *top*, 33, 34, 35, 38, 39, 40 *top*, 41 *top*, 48 *top*;
Government of Alberta: 57 *bottom right*;
Sonia Halliday: 12 *centre left*;
Kit Houghton: 6 *top right*, 18 *bottom*, 19, 20 *top*, 25 *bottom*, 36 *centre right*, 42 *left*, 47 *top*

and bottom right, 48 bottom right, 49 bottom left, 51 bottom;
Irish Tourist Board: 18 *top*;
E. D. Lacey: 28 *bottom right*, 44 *centre*, 45, 46 *top and bottom*, 50, 41 *top*, 52 *bottom*, 53 *top and bottom*, 59 *bottom*;
Mansell Collection: 14 *centre*;
Metropolitan Police: 54 *bottom*;
National Gallery, London: 10
Post Office: 55 *bottom right*;
Sally Anne Thompson Animal Photography Ltd: 14 *bottom*, 16, 17, 23 *top*, 28 *centre*, 31 *bottom*, 36 *top and bottom left*, 41 *bottom*;

S.A.T.O.U.R.: 44 *top*;
Zefa: 4, 6 *bottom*, 7 *top*, 9, 11, 12, 15, 17 *bottom left*, 28 *bottom left*, 36 *centre right*, 40 *bottom*, 42-43, 44 *bottom and centre*, 45, 47 *top left*, 52 *top*, 53 *centre*, 54 *top left*, 55 *top*, 56 *top left*, 57 *top right*, 58 *bottom*;

Picture research: Jacqueline Cookson and Penny Warn.

The author wishes to thank those who over many years and in several different ways have contributed to this book. In particular he acknowledges help from: Miss Penny Herrington, John Howard; Miss Marion King; Deborah Manley; John Richards; Mrs Diana Scott; Stewart Scott; Miss Ann Stone and the Poplar Grove Riding and Training Establishment.

About this book

This is a book for all who love horses and ponies. It is a book for those who ride and those who want to ride. It sets out to give a comprehensive picture of this most noble of animals both at work and play.

Some people want to know about breeds or the way a horse or pony moves through its different paces. Others want to improve their jumping technique or know about competitive riding. Eventing, including dressage and cross-country riding, is explained, as are other sporting activities for the horse and rider. Of equal importance to horse lovers is a knowledge of how to look after a horse and the essential routine of stable management.

Although this book is intended for the younger person, there is much here to interest every age group. It is a book for all horse lovers throughout the world and will, it is hoped, give lasting pleasure to the many who own, ride, or who long for the day when they will have a horse or pony of their own.

Below: Freedom, entertainment, labour, sport, friendship. All these are given by horses and ponies to people. Together horses and humans conquered the world. And even now when machines have taken over from the draught animal, the horse still contributes enormously to the pleasure of living.

Points of the Horse

One of the earliest lessons for those who ride, or those who are interested in the world of horses and ponies, should deal with the various parts of the horse. These are known as the 'points of the horse', and are common to all breeds and types.

It is surprising how often the points are referred to. Of course, they continually appear in manuals of riding and are constantly heard during every period of instruction!

Considering Conformation
Although the points are often being discussed, they must also be looked at together with the more complicated subject of 'conformation'. 'Conformation' means 'shape' or the way a horse or pony is 'put together'. Unless we know the points, therefore, we can hardly talk about the shape or form of a horse.

How, for example, would we explain what we know to be strong quarters if we did not know where the quarters are? And could we describe what we mean when we say a horse has a hollow back?

Below: This horse has been created by the artist to be rejected. It exhibits many of the points of bad conformation, It shows a ewe neck, where the crest is concave and not convex. Its back is too long, and the overall body shape is bad. The legs are not good and 'boxy' hoofs and pigeon toes must be avoided. Also avoid a horse with hocks that turn inwards. This is known as being 'cow-hocked'.

Right: Not all the 'points of the horse' are shown on this illustration. A more detailed list can be found in books which specialize in the subject of breeding and the care of the horse. The points listed here are the ones most frequently used.

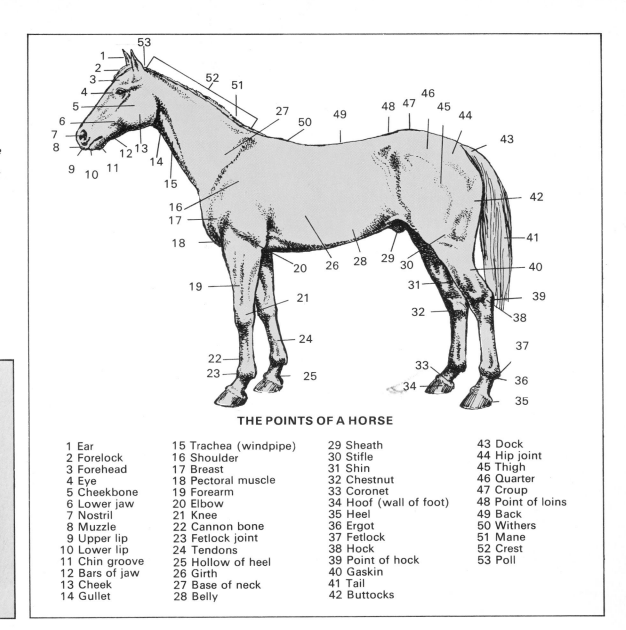

THE POINTS OF A HORSE

1 Ear	15 Trachea (windpipe)	29 Sheath	43 Dock
2 Forelock	16 Shoulder	30 Stifle	44 Hip joint
3 Forehead	17 Breast	31 Shin	45 Thigh
4 Eye	18 Pectoral muscle	32 Chestnut	46 Quarter
5 Cheekbone	19 Forearm	33 Coronet	47 Croup
6 Lower jaw	20 Elbow	34 Hoof (wall of foot)	48 Point of loins
7 Nostril	21 Knee	35 Heel	49 Back
8 Muzzle	22 Cannon bone	36 Ergot	50 Withers
9 Upper lip	23 Fetlock joint	37 Fetlock	51 Mane
10 Lower lip	24 Tendons	38 Hock	52 Crest
11 Chin groove	25 Hollow of heel	39 Point of hock	53 Poll
12 Bars of jaw	26 Girth	40 Gaskin	
13 Cheek	27 Base of neck	41 Tail	
14 Gullet	28 Belly	42 Buttocks	

The height of a horse or pony is measured in 'hands'. One hand is 100 mm (4 ins) or the average width of a man's hand. The measurement is made from the highest point of the withers to the ground, allowing 1 cm ($\frac{1}{2}$ in) if the horse is shod. A horse stands at a height of more than 14·2 hands. Other than in certain showing classes, where heights are accepted up to 15 hands, ponies are measured from 14·2 hands downwards. Draught horses can stand up to 20 hands high. The tallest recorded horses were 21·1 hands (2·16 metres).

What should be looked for when a horse or pony is considered as having good or bad conformation? All who ride, and many who don't, know at first sight that one horse looks better than another, even though they may not be able to explain their reasons for such a judgement. In their minds they probably compare proportion, shape and form. And that is part of the judgement one makes when considering conformation.

Sharing any specialist knowledge is important, and if we have been fortunate in acquiring knowledge about the world of horses and about the points we should use such knowledge well.

When you are choosing a horse, you would be wise to consult a vet, for although a horse or pony may have some bad points, they need not necessarily deter you from buying it.

To examine conformation it is necessary to look at a horse from all sides. The picture on the right, however, shows several very good points. The head is in proportion to the body and the eyes are set wide. The ears would indicate alertness. The neck is set well into the shoulders, and the horse's back is in excellent proportion. The muscular and rounded quarters are another indication of good conformation. The pasterns are neither too short nor too large, and the hoofs and feet are 'clean'. All-in-all this is a most beautifully 'put together' animal.

Above: A brown horse is a dark brown colour all over with brown mane and tail. Sometimes there is a trace of black in the brown, though brown is the dominant colour.

Above: A chestnut horse has a reddish-brown body with mane and tail of similar colour. There are three shades of chestnut, described as dark, liver and light.

Above: A black horse has a black body with black tail and mane. No other colour is accepted on a truly black horse other than white markings.

Above: A bay horse has a brown body with black mane and tail. Invariably some black appears on the limbs of a bay horse.

Below: In a dun horse the body colour will vary from cream to a kind of yellow. Most duns have a black line running along the back and black manes and tails.

Below: There are three shades of roan: strawberry, bay and blue. A strawberry roan is chestnut with a mixture of white hairs. A bay roan (or red roan) has a bay-based colour with white hairs, giving it a reddish appearance. A blue roan has a black or brown body colour, white hairs giving it a bluish look.

Colours

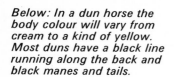

The principal colours of horses and ponies are black, brown, bay and chestnut. Other colours and mixes of colour are known, but these, like grey, are not true colours but the result of pigment failure.

During the first year of a horse's life the body colour changes and not until the second year will the 'true' colour appear. Consider an almost black foal. Nearly always the black coat will turn grey, a mixture of black and white hairs. Such horses will, as they grow older, develop more white, though white is not a colour used to describe a horse.

The colour and other markings of each young horse or pony must be accurately recorded to establish identification. But, even in an older animal, the colour is not always clearly recognizable. If in doubt, examine the hairs in the muzzle or around the eyes. The colour there will be decisive.

Many of the colours accredited to horses and ponies are universally adopted, though several of the names of odd colours are peculiar to individual countries.

Below: Cream horses have a cream coloured coat with unpigmented skin. The eyes of a cream horse are pinkish.

Below: A piebald horse has a coat of irregular shapes and patches of black and white. A skewbald, on the other hand, has large and irregular patches of brown and white or white with any colour other than black.

Below: The coat of a grey horse has a mixture of black and grey-white hairs.

Markings

A horse or pony with no visible markings is known as 'whole-coloured'. The great majority of horses, however, have some markings on their heads or limbs. Some of these markings are shown here. A variety of markings may also appear on the body. A flecked horse has small collections of white hairs spread irregularly over its body. A horse with zebra marks has stripes on the neck, withers, quarters or limbs. A patch describes larger and well-defined areas of contrasting colour. It should not be confused with the colours of a skewbald or piebald horse.

Markings of the Head

Star: a white mark on the forehead.
Blaze: a broad white mark which runs down the face, usually spreading as it nears the muzzle.
Stripe: a narrow white line down the face.
White face: white covering the forehead and area around the eyes, nose and parts of the muzzle.
Snip: a white mark between the nostrils.
Wall eye: a white or blue-white appearance in the eye due to lack of pigment in the iris.

MARKINGS ON THE LEGS

Below: Markings on the legs of horses and ponies are known by the area they cover. On the left is a leg showing a full stocking (1).

Next, from left, are white fetlocks (2); white coronets (3), and white pasterns (4). White heels (5) are quite rare.

White socks (6) cover the fetlock, but reach higher than the area known as white fetlocks. A white stocking on one leg (7).

An old saying goes:
One white foot, ride him for your life;
Two white feet, give him to your wife;
Three white feet, give him to your man;
Four white feet, sell him if you can!

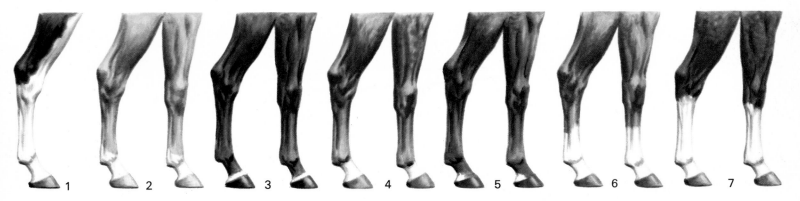

Breeds and Breeding

Above from left: Four types of horse: a pony; a light horse suitable for most equestrian activities; a heavy horse with a rather exaggerated gait, and a draught horse built for heavy work on farms or for pulling heavy loads.

Horses are divided by type and breed. They are grouped in types according to their size and purpose: light horses, heavy horses, ponies, polo ponies, cobs and so on. There are different types of each breed. For example, some Palominos are light horses, some are ponies.

The aim of animal breeding is to produce the best specimens of any type or breed. It is a maxim of breeding that 'to produce the best you must have the best from which to breed'. Yet, having the best sire or dam will not ensure that they will pass on to their progeny only that which is good, and never pass on any of their faults!

There are possibly three hundred breeds of horses and ponies in the world. Each breed has its own breed society. In Great Britain the societies which hold registers include: Arabs, Anglo-Arabs, Hackneys, Shires, Cleveland Bays, and all the nine British native pony breeds. Thoroughbreds, which were developed from the Arab, are separately recorded in the General Stud Book. When pure-bred (that is bred directly from horses of the same breed), a horse or pony can be recorded in the Stud Register of that breed society. In some societies a register is kept of part-bred stock (that is horses descending from a crossing of breeds), but this is not common.

The right horse for you

If you own a part-bred, or one of the types, you do not have a 'wrong' horse or pony. Hunters, as such, are a breed of horse, but many people who hunt do not ride a pure-bred. What is important is that you have the right horse or pony for *you*. Whatever the breeding, a horse will only give the owner or rider true pleasure when everything is done to see that he is properly looked after and cared for.

When the time comes to choose your own horse or pony, you must ask and answer several questions. To what use do you want to put him? Do you want a show jumper, an eventer, a horse for showing or just for riding? How do you plan to keep him? Will he be kept at grass? How much time can you devote to him each day? How well can you ride? And have you any experience in looking after a horse?

Left, above: An engraving, made in 1823, of the Darley Arabian. This horse was brought to England by Richard Darley in 1704. It was to become, with the Godolphin Arabian and the Byerley Turk—two other imported Arabians—one of the founder sires of the Thoroughbred. The Darley Arabian stood at 15 hands. He was a pure-bred Arabian of the Managhi strain.

Left: A beautifully proportioned Arab.

Successful breeding is very involved and requires great skill. In pure-bred horse breeding there is a continual search for perfection. There are several systems of breeding. Breeding from stallions related to the mares is known as inbreeding. Breeding from unrelated stallions is known as outbreeding. In grading up the mares of one generation, not necessarily pure-bred, are bred to pure-bred stallions. In cross-breeding the pure-bred mares of one type are bred to pure-bred stallions of another type. Whatever the system the horse breeder must set immensely high standards.

Above right: The American Palomino is not yet strictly a breed. The Palomino Breed Society reckon that it will take a few more generations before this horse will always breed true. It is a golden-brown horse with a cream or silvery mane and tail.

Right: The forebears of the Icelandic pony probably came to the island with Norwegian or Irish settlers. They are stocky little animals, standing 12 to 13 hands high, with thick manes. They have to be extremely hardy to survive in the cold northern climate.

The picture below shows a delightful scene of mares with a foal.

1 ▲

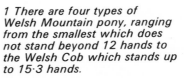

2 ▲

3 ▲   ▼ 4

1 There are four types of Welsh Mountain pony, ranging from the smallest which does not stand beyond 12 hands to the Welsh Cob which stands up to 15·3 hands.

2 The Exmoor is perhaps the oldest of the British native breeds. It is a small breed, standing usually up to 12·2 hands. The Exmoor is a most intelligent and honest pony and will carry weights beyond all proportion to its size.

3 The American Thoroughbred breed can be traced to stallions bred from foundation sires of the English Thoroughbred. In 1730 a foal of the Darley Arabian, Bulle Rocke, was sent to Virginia. From this early stock America today produces some of the finest Thoroughbreds in the world.

4 A hunter is bred to carry a rider over all types of country. Hunters are sometimes from Thoroughbred stock, but usually are cross-bred to produce a safe, intelligent, and courageous ride.

5 The Danish Knabstrub is descended from a spotted mare said to have been taken to Denmark by a Spanish officer during the Napoleonic Wars. Knabstrubs are specially noted for speed and hardiness.

6 From the Shetland Islands to the north of Scotland comes the smallest pony of all pony breeds. They are measured in inches rather than hands and the maximum height allowed, if a Shetland is to be registered in the official Stud Book, is 42 inches (1·06m).

7 The Connemara, with its Spanish influence, has become well-loved as a family pony. They are sturdy, reliable and highly intelligent. It stands between 13 and 14·2 hands.

8 The Morgan was named after the founder of the breed, Justin Morgan. It is claimed that the Morgan has both Thoroughbred and Arab blood in its veins. Bays, browns and blacks are the most common colours.

9 The Lipizzaner horses of the Spanish Riding School in Vienna are world renowned. Mostly grey, the Lipizzaner is at its best when performing haute ecole (high school).

10 The ancestors of the Hanoverian were the Great German Horse, the war horse of the Middle Ages, crossed later with the English Thoroughbred.

11 The Breton, a light draught horse, has alertness combined with immense stamina.

5 ▼

6 ▲

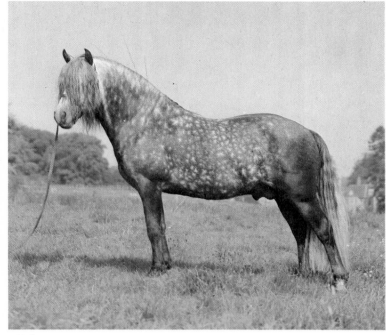

7 ▲

8 ▲

▼9   10 ▲

▼11

Buying a Horse or Pony

Above: A common method of buying and selling a horse or pony is through a market. But this is not advised for those with little or no experience of what to look for. Horses can also be bought at sales which are held regularly at major racecourses and equestrian centres.

Below: A delightful family scene showing a pony changing hands now that the earlier rider has outgrown the animal. The new owner, the little girl seen making friends with the pony, is obviously excited by all that is going on. Buying a pony from a rider who has outgrown the animal is one of the better methods for the inexperienced. It is likely the pony's ability and temperament will have been known for some time.

There are several ways of setting out to buy a horse or pony. These vary from country to country. In parts of Europe horses are seldom advertised in the papers. In Britain and the United States this method is perhaps the most widely used. Horse sales, usually held on market days, are practically unknown in some countries; in others this is the common way of buying and selling.

Nobody should attempt to buy a horse or pony for the first time without talking about it with someone with experience. Finding the ideal horse is never simple. It may take a considerable time. In all probability you will have to travel hundreds of miles and look at many different types, breeds, colours and heights before finding the animal you are seeking.

Even when you have advertised your requirements and detailed the breed, height, age and experience you seek, you may still find that many photographs sent by prospective sellers have been quite misleading when you see the actual horse. As a buyer you must be patient. Wait for the veterinary surgeon's report on the condition of the animal before agreeing to purchase.

Before you buy your first horse or pony take every opportunity to learn about what it means to look after it. Help a friend or spend time at a riding school. Make sure you can answer these questions satisfactorily. Do you have the facilities for keeping a pony? What do you need to ensure that your stabling and grazing is suitable? Do you understand stable management? Do you fully understand how to feed a pony?

Before you take on the responsibility of caring for your own horse, there is a great deal to learn and a great deal to do.

WHAT HEIGHT TO BUY

When buying for the first time many people wonder whether there is a 'right' size of pony for a child of a particular age. There can be no firm guide, since not all children are of the same height or weight. And some children will have had little or no experience of riding.

A buyer must also consider the use to which the pony is to be put. Will he be required for showing? Is he being bought for hacking and for quiet riding? Will he be kept at grass, and will he be kept in the country or in a town? There are many things to think about. And these are further reasons why experienced help should be sought by those new to horses and ponies.

Taking a boy or girl of average height and weight the following is a *very rough* guide to the correct height of pony:

age of rider	height of pony
under 7 years	up to 11 hands
7 to 9	11 to 12·2 hands
9 to 12	12·2 to 13·2 hands
12 to 14	13·2 to 14·2 hands
14 to 16	perhaps the rider will now be out of pony classes and will require a horse, say up to 15·2 hands.

The Veterinary Surgeon

A veterinary surgeon is qualified to give medical and surgical treatment to animals.

Although much of a vet's time will be taken up with diagnosing and treating sick animals, he (or she) is continually doing all he can to *prevent* illness.

Technological advances in X-rays and highly specialized operating techniques, with the additional support of sophisticated machines, drugs and vaccines, mean the vet must keep his skills continually up to date. The problems he will face vary from country to country and from one climate to another. The training is long and hard, and in some countries the educational standards required for entry to veterinary college are higher than those asked for by some medical schools.

The veterinary surgeon will spend much of the day examining, diagnosing and treating all manner of sickness in a variety of animal life, including farm stock, pets, and horses. Veterinary assistants undertake the more routine work carried out in the dispensary and laboratory.

A vet will always be in attendance at race meetings and at most horse shows and equestrian events. On these occasions a judge or official can call for a veterinary examination should there be doubts about the soundness of a horse.

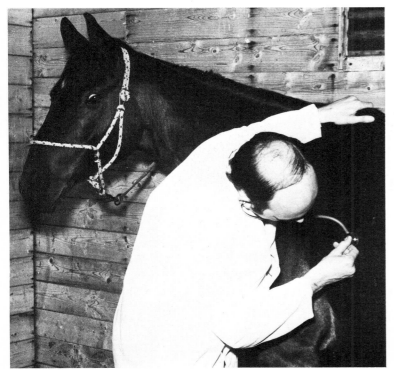

Above: A vet checking the horse's legs. He can feel signs of weakness and can tell if there have been any previous serious injuries. This is something the inexperienced can never do. No vet will pass a horse as fit if the legs are unsound.

Among the signs of a healthy pony are:

He will feed up well.

He will be alert and interested in all that goes on around him.

He will stand squarely on all four legs.

He will obey the aids given by the rider, when these are applied correctly.

He will be seen to enjoy his work and periods of rest.

Left: The stethoscope is used much as it is by a doctor—to hear the sounds in the chest and other parts of the body. It is important for the vet to know the condition of the horse's breathing and the state of his lungs and heart.

COMMON AILMENTS

Many common ailments found in horses and ponies can be treated in the stable. But never hesitate to call your vet if you are in any doubt.

All stables should have a special place for a medicine cabinet. A smaller medicine box should be to hand in a horse box or trailer.

In the *Manual of Horsemanship,* published by the British Horse Society, there is a list of suggested contents for a medicine cabinet. Here is part of that list:

A pair of blunt ended 10 cm (4 in) surgical scissors. Some calico bandages. Several rolls of cotton wool. A few packets of lint. A roll or two of gamgee or other tissue. Small packets of oiled silk. One or two colic drinks from your vet. A bottle of embrocation. Some witch hazel and a tin of kaolin. A jar of cough electuary. A tin or 'puffer' of antibiotic dusting powder. A jar or tin of common salt or Epsom salts. A bottle of glycerine.

The contents of the medicine cabinet should be checked regularly. Items used must immediately be replaced.

Left: A horse's mouth is easy and safe to open, despite what some people think! By examining the teeth an experienced person can quickly assess the approximate age of the horse.

Bottom: The 'action' of a horse or pony is most important. A vet can check this by asking the horse to be walked away and then returned on a straight line.

THE AGE OF A HORSE

The age of a horse or pony is determined by the shape and marks found on the teeth. The diagram here will help you younger rider to make a check.
Below: Milk teeth appear approximately 10 days after birth. The teeth then develop with marked characteristics

until the horse or pony reaches the age of 15. It then becomes more difficult to determine the exact age.
At 2 years most horses begin to show dark rings on the biting edges of their teeth.
From the age of 5 a 'full mouth' of permanent teeth is found.

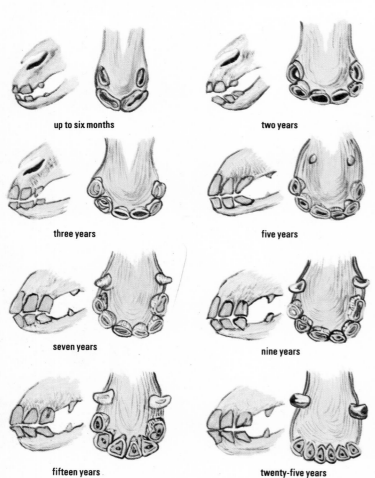

up to six months

two years

three years

five years

seven years

nine years

fifteen years

twenty-five years

When you are buying a horse

Once you have seen the horse or pony you think suits your needs (and it is always best if someone with considerable experience is with you) you must, before buying, have the animal examined by a veterinary surgeon. Some sellers will insist this is done; others will try to tell you that it is unnecessary. It does not matter how well you know the horse, or how often you have watched him perform, seek an independent and professional assessment.

Just as a doctor, by examination, can determine the general state of a patient's health, so the veterinary surgeon, by undertaking a series of checks, is able to give an opinion as to the soundness of a horse or pony.

One of the first things the vet is likely to do on meeting the horse for the first time is to test its lungs and pulse. He will then ask that the horse be trotted or cantered for a time before he makes a second examination. The rate of breathing and the condition of the animal's heart show much about the horse's overall state of health.

Next, the vet will look closely at the horse's head and examine its eyes. He will look at the teeth to determine its age. The vet will also pay particular attention to the feet, and will feel up each leg for signs of splints (a bony growth) or other weaknesses. He will then examine the soles of each foot. Finally, he will want to see the horse's action and will ask that it is led away and trotted from him for a short distance, and then be turned around and brought back again.

The vet then usually discusses the horse in general terms, giving his opinion, before preparing a written report.

Stable Management

Looking after a horse or pony means far more than seeing that he is well fed, watered and groomed. No horse or pony is happy when left for long periods. They love companionship and look forward to your visits.

A daily routine and inspection is essential to ensure your horse's well-being, whether he is grass-kept or stable-kept. You should inspect him first thing each day. This is a duty which is more important than giving the first feed or 'mucking out'. Once you are certain there are no signs of lameness or other signs that all is not well, the work of 'stable management' is begun.

Stable management must never be thought of as a chore. Caring for a horse or pony, and seeing that all you do is thorough and complete, can give immense satisfaction.

Sometimes there is more work to be done when horses are out at grass. The fences and hedges must be checked to see that they are sound. The state of the field must be watched to see that it is not over-grazed. Plants which are dangerous when eaten to excess must be removed. The fields and the shelter must be kept clean and droppings cleared to the muck heap. Even more important is a constant check of the drinking trough.

All this demands time. There are no short cuts if you have your horse's welfare at heart.

In the Stable

Possibly it is easier to look after a stable-kept horse since balanced feeds can be given at regular times. And the horse is always there for inspection and grooming which is not always the case with those kept at grass! But the stable-kept horse must have regular exercise and, where possible, a time to graze.

Feeding your horse or pony

Grass-kept horses or ponies who are asked to undertake even gentle work will, at times, require their grazing to be supplemented with a feed of hay. Protein can be given in the form of pony nuts, and additional feeds can be given which may include vitamins, linseed, bran, corn and chaff.

In the autumn and winter months, when there is little nutritious value in the grazing, the pony will need larger amounts of hay. In the springtime, when the grazing is fresh and lush, you must watch carefully to see that your pony is not over-feeding. It is sometimes best if the pony is brought in for part of the day and allowed out to graze for shorter periods.

Proper feeding is very, very important. If you are in doubt Ask your veterinary surgeon whether or not your horse is in good condition and what you should do about him.

It is almost impossible to find the perfect stable area. Owners have their ideas as to how this should be laid out. Much will depend on the site, the position of a roadway, the access to the paddocks, and the number of horses or ponies being stabled. On the right is a plan suitable for the keeping of three horses.

Note the position of the feed store and hay and bedding stores in relation to the 'muck-heap'. Keep the siting of a muck-heap away from the stables, but make sure it can be emptied without difficulty.

An ideal yard must have good drainage. The plan suggests a line of drains are placed near to the roadside boundary. This is both necessary for ensuring that the yard can be kept clean, and is essential in some areas to comply with local bye-laws.

At all times the yard, loose-boxes and stores must be neat and tidy. There is nothing more distressing than the sight of a dirty and untidy stable area. Cleanliness, and therefore hygiene, must be the watchword.

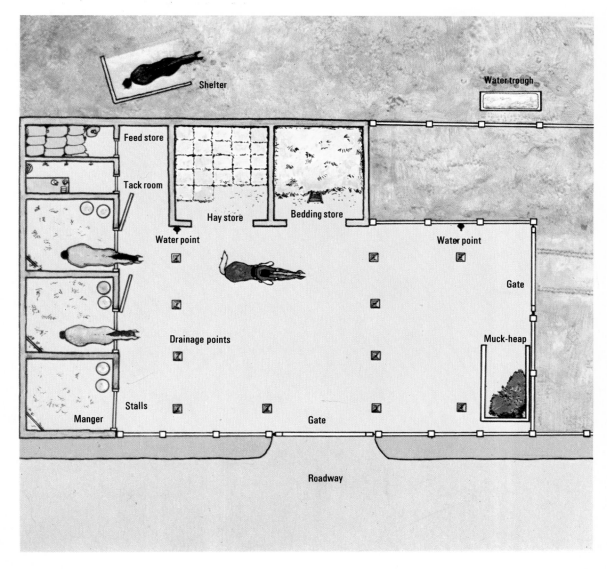

Shelter · Water trough · Feed store · Tack room · Hay store · Bedding store · Water point · Water point · Gate · Drainage points · Muck-heap · Stalls · Manger · Gate · Roadway

Above: It is not advisable to use barbed wire in fields where horses or ponies are kept. All boundary fences must be checked regularly, and care must be taken to see that any broken wires are repaired immediately.

Right: Check that the ball-cock is allowing a flow of fresh water into the trough.

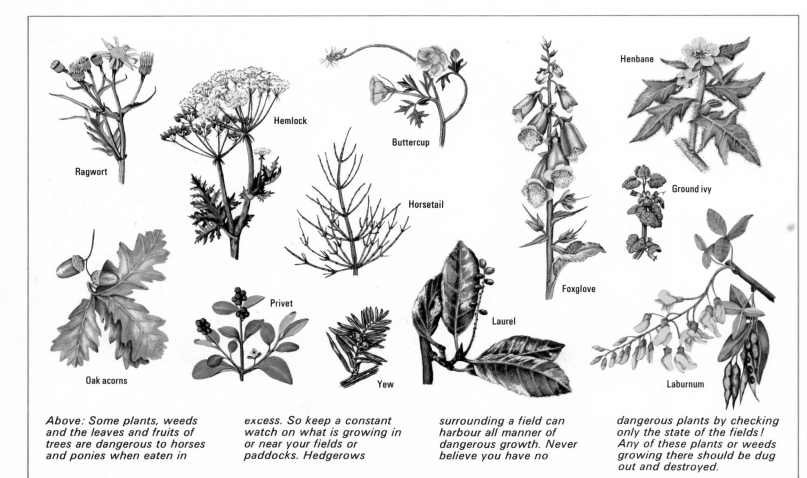

Ragwort

Hemlock

Buttercup

Henbane

Horsetail

Foxglove

Ground ivy

Oak acorns

Privet

Yew

Laurel

Laburnum

Above: Some plants, weeds and the leaves and fruits of trees are dangerous to horses and ponies when eaten in *excess. So keep a constant watch on what is growing in or near your fields or paddocks. Hedgerows* *surrounding a field can harbour all manner of dangerous growth. Never believe you have no* *dangerous plants by checking only the state of the fields! Any of these plants or weeds growing there should be dug out and destroyed.*

Right: Soiled straw should be removed with a light fork. This is separated from the dry bedding and removed with the manure to the 'muck-heap'. Mucking out must be done every morning. As long as the horse is tied up and has his morning hay net, he will stand quietly while you get on with the job.

A LAME HORSE

Should your horse become lame you will first have to find out which leg is causing the trouble. Trot him quietly on an even surface to see if it is a fore or hind leg. Then you must find out which part of the leg is causing the distress. Feel up and along each leg. Compare signs of swelling with a leg you think is sound. Excessive heat in any part of the leg indicates something wrong. See that no stones have got lodged between the frog and the shoe. Check the shoes and clenches. If the horse's foot has been bruised by coming down on a sharp object, it will be tender to the touch. Never trust your first judgement. Check again. Then do all you can to make your horse comfortable.

Right: Part of a clean and tidy-looking tack room. Note how neatly the cleaned saddles are arranged. In the background are some bridles. These too have been cleaned thoroughly and made ready for use. All items of saddlery are expensive and they must be treated with care. In a tack room there should be a place set aside for each item of equipment, from bandages, leathers, reins, stirrups and girths to the larger items such as saddles, bridles and rugs.

Care of tack

Cleaning tack can be an enjoyable task if it is done properly. Saddlery and other equipment is expensive to buy and replace, but with care can last several years. Regular cleaning is the key to preservation, and cleaning means more than just wiping the saddle with a damp cloth or sponge and occasionally washing the bits!

Before cleaning, the leathers and girth must be removed from the saddle, and each part of the bridle taken down. Stirrups should be separated from the leathers.

Then all parts of the leather should be washed. A bucket of warm water is essential. Never use very hot water or soda when cleaning leather. The water should be clean and free from additives.

Next, apply saddle soap, which must be polished off with a clean sponge and dried with a leather. In addition to its cleaning properties, saddle soap puts back many of the ingredients necessary to keep the leather in good condition. Leather, once it becomes dry, tends to crack. When this happens some people apply olive oil, glycerine, dubbin or other substances to make the leather supple. But with regular cleaning with a good saddle soap this should not be necessary.

Check your tack

While you are cleaning the tack, take a good look at the stitching. Make sure none of it is showing signs of wear or is becoming loose. Check the bits for any rough edges. It is important for the safety of both horse and rider that all buckles are secure.

Bits, stirrup irons and metal buckles should be washed in clean water and thoroughly dried. Should any sign of rust appear, apply a metal polish, but polish it off before using the tack or putting it away.

Above: A bucket of clean water, some saddle soap and two sponges—and plenty of elbow-grease—are important if the saddle is to be thoroughly cleaned.

Below: Some of the items which form part of a grooming kit.

Grooming

The object of grooming is to promote health, maintain condition, prevent disease, improve appearance and to ensure cleanliness. It must never be looked upon as a routine or chore, since it makes a great contribution to the well-being and fitness of the horse or pony.

Practically all horse lovers know how to set about grooming, but there are differences in the grooming of horses kept at grass from those stable-kept.

Below: One of the sponges must be kept for cleaning the eyes and muzzle of the horse.

Water brush Dandy brush

Body brush

Hoof-pick Curry comb

Comb

Stable rubber

Cleaning material with sponge and duster

A horse at grass must never have all the grease removed from his coat by heavy treatment with a body brush. During the winter months a horse must retain a certain amount of grease, for without it he can lose protection and body warmth. When the weather is severe, it is best to concentrate the grooming on a daily brushing down with a dandy brush, removing caked mud and dirt. In all weathers, the eyes, muzzle and dock area must be kept clean.

The Grooming Kit

The stable-kept horse demands full daily attention. Each item in the grooming kit must be used thoroughly and purposefully.

When looking at a grooming kit remember that:
  the *hoof pick* is used for cleaning out the feet;
  the *dandy brush* is needed for removing caked mud, heavy dirt and dust;
  the *body brush* will remove dust, scurf, dandruff and grease from the coat, mane and tail;
  the *curry comb*, whether metal or rubber, is used for cleaning the body brush;
  the *water brush,* when dampened, is used on the mane, tail and feet;
  the *sponges* (there should be at least two) are used with clean water (a) to clean the eyes, muzzle, and (b) the dock;
  the *wisp* promotes circulation and helps tone up the muscles;
  the *stable rubber* adds a final polish.

Below: This horse, without a headcollar, is being asked to come to hand by being offered some pony nuts.

Above: Remove the head collar and place it round the horse's neck before brushing the horse's head.

The Farrier

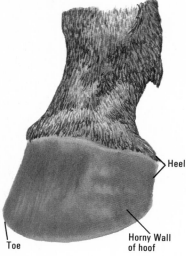

Heel

Toe

Horny Wall of hoof

Bars

Frog

Sole

Wall

The old saying 'no foot, no horse' is as true today as it ever was. A horse or pony without sound feet is, sadly, a useless and unhappy animal. When a horse's feet are neglected it is a slow process to full recovery and normal action. Not even the blacksmith, or farrier, with all his skill, can suddenly put things right. There is, of course, much he can do, but the responsibility for seeing that a horse or pony is fit for work, especially where the feet are concerned, is that of the person looking after him.

Going to the farrier is not a question of waiting until the shoes have become worn or lost (cast). At frequent intervals (perhaps as often as every six to eight weeks) the old shoes should be removed and the walls of the feet trimmed back. The walls grow fast and, where a pony is not working much, they can quickly outgrow the shoes. And that is where the danger lies. Unless the growth is cut back, the horse will go lame. Neglected feet upset the horse's balance and cause strain to the ligaments, joints and tendons.

The feet of every horse or pony must be checked once a day. Use the hoof pick to clean around the frog and examine the sole of the foot. Check the shoes to see that they have not become worn so that sharp edges have formed. These can cut the horse's other legs. Make sure no clenches have risen.

When you take your pony to the farrier, listen to his advice. And each time you watch a horse or pony being shod, think back through the centuries to the men who have carried out their craft with skill, patience and an understanding of the horse.

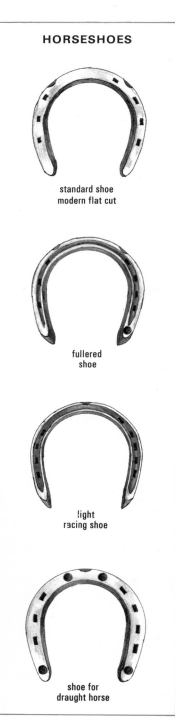

HORSESHOES

standard shoe
modern flat cut

fullered
shoe

light
racing shoe

shoe for
draught horse

The farrier brings the heated shoe to the anvil and shapes it by using either a 'cross pin' or 'cat's head' hammer. Next the nail holes are made with a 'stamp', a tool with a sharpened end the size of the heads of the nails he will be using to nail on the shoe.

The farrier first knocks up, or cuts off, the clenches with a hammer and the end of his buffer. The shoe is then tapped until it can be lifted by the pincers.

Starting at the heel, the old shoe is levered off by pulling it down towards the toe. This is slow work, since great care must be taken not to damage the wall of the foot.

Once the old shoe has been removed, dirt and remaining bits are cleaned from the foot with the blunt side of the 'searcher' or drawing knife.

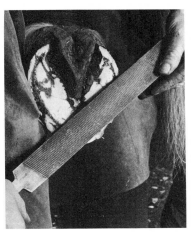

Finally the foot is rasped flat and level to ensure an equal distribution of weight on all parts of the foot, when the shoe has been fitted.

When the new shoe has been made, it will be taken from the fire by means of a 'pritchel' and placed on the foot. The horse feels no discomfort or pain. Having scorched the foot, the clips are cut out in the wall.

If the shoe does not fit, it will be taken back to the anvil to be adjusted. The shoe is then cooled and the nail holes checked to make certain the shape and fit are accurate.

The new shoe is nailed on with the driving hammer—starting at the toe so that the shoe can be moved to its correct position. The inside nails are hammered in first. The final one will be that at the outside of the heel.

The protruding nail can be seen in this picture. The farrier will have made seven nail holes in the shoe, four on the outside edge and three on the inside edge.

The nails are next tightened up by placing the pincers under the ends of the nails (the clenches). These are 'wrung off' and each nail is hammered tightly home.

The 'clenches' are turned over and tapped into the wall of the foot. Finally, the outside of the wall is rasped to make sure there are no sharp edges.

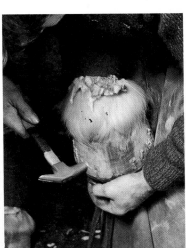

Right: Oakwood Zaltah, a magnificent 6-year-old black horse was sired by an Anglo-Arab from a Russian mare. He stands at 16·2 hands, and is owned and ridden by Miss Ann Stone.

She is using an All-purpose or General-purpose saddle, suitable for a number of different equestrian activities including hunting, hacking, jumping and eventing.

Below: A young rider with a show saddle. The saddle has a cut-away part to show to best advantage the shoulders of the pony.

Below left: This cowboy has a Western saddle. Note the length of his stirrups contrasted with those on the other saddles.

Below, right: A racing saddle is light in weight and has a small saddle flap. Jockeys ride with very short stirrup leathers.

Saddlery

The word 'saddlery' conjures up for most of us the basic items used in riding: saddles, bridles, bits and reins. But the word has a far greater meaning. It covers those other items of equipment which clothe the horse and enable the rider to maintain control.

Two important points must be emphasized about saddlery: all saddlery and equipment *must be safe* and *must fit*. This may seem obvious, but it is a sad fact that many horses are ridden in ill-fitting saddlery. It is essential, if you are to expect a horse to perform freely and without undue resistance, that the equipment he is carrying is comfortable.

Today with such a variety of choice, it is not easy to decide what to buy, even if you are replacing a piece of saddlery which is broken or badly worn. It is much safer to consult a saddler. Tell him what you think you need; then take the advice he gives. Saddlery is expensive and it is a wise investment to have it *right* at the beginning.

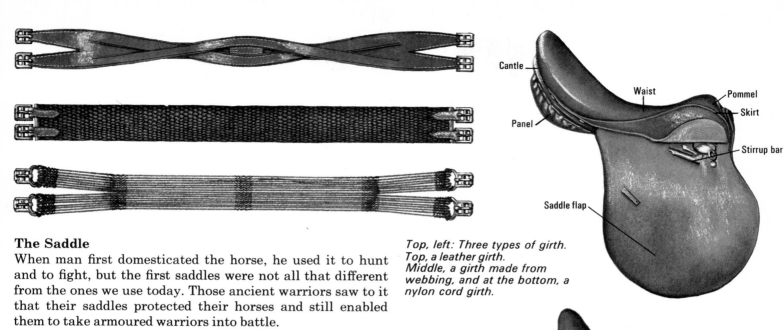

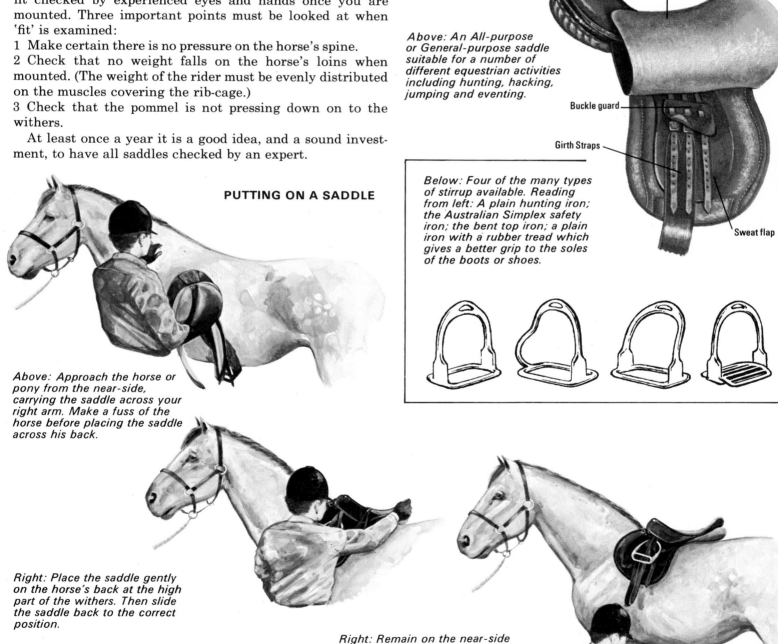

The Saddle

When man first domesticated the horse, he used it to hunt and to fight, but the first saddles were not all that different from the ones we use today. Those ancient warriors saw to it that their saddles protected their horses and still enabled them to take armoured warriors into battle.

Although when you put on a saddle it is possible to check the fit, it is good practice every now and again to have the fit checked by experienced eyes and hands once you are mounted. Three important points must be looked at when 'fit' is examined:

1 Make certain there is no pressure on the horse's spine.

2 Check that no weight falls on the horse's loins when mounted. (The weight of the rider must be evenly distributed on the muscles covering the rib-cage.)

3 Check that the pommel is not pressing down on to the withers.

At least once a year it is a good idea, and a sound investment, to have all saddles checked by an expert.

PUTTING ON A SADDLE

Top, left: Three types of girth. Top, a leather girth. Middle, a girth made from webbing, and at the bottom, a nylon cord girth.

Above: An All-purpose or General-purpose saddle suitable for a number of different equestrian activities including hunting, hacking, jumping and eventing.

Below: Four of the many types of stirrup available. Reading from left: A plain hunting iron; the Australian Simplex safety iron; the bent top iron; a plain iron with a rubber tread which gives a better grip to the soles of the boots or shoes.

Above: Approach the horse or pony from the near-side, carrying the saddle across your right arm. Make a fuss of the horse before placing the saddle across his back.

Right: Place the saddle gently on the horse's back at the high part of the withers. Then slide the saddle back to the correct position.

Right: Remain on the near-side and take the girth from under the horse's belly and buckle up. Once this is done the stirrups can be 'run down'.

29

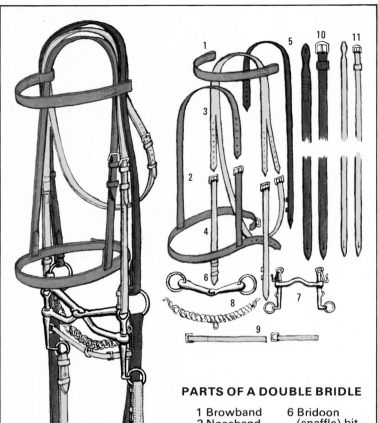

PARTS OF A DOUBLE BRIDLE

1 Browband
2 Noseband
3 Headpiece
4 Cheek-pieces
5 Bridoon cheek and sliphead

6 Bridoon (snaffle) bit
7 Weymouth (curb) bit
8 Curb chain
9 Lip strap
10 Snaffle reins
11 Curb reins

Right: The first horse has a headcollar, which is used for leading it or tying it up. The other horses are wearing three different types of bridle. The choice of bridle will depend on the rider's experience, the horse's temperament and the purpose for which it is being ridden.

Headcollar

The Bridle

The function of the bridle is to support the bit, which, with correct use of the reins, is the main control a rider has on a horse or pony.

The most commonly used bridles are the *snaffle*, the *Weymouth* or *Double Bridle* and the *Pelham*.

The snaffle is the gentlest bridle. It is therefore recommended for younger or novice riders. It uses a single bit which may be in one piece (similar to the snaffle opposite) or jointed (like the Eggbutt snaffle). These bits help to raise the horse's head.

PUTTING ON A BRIDLE

Left: Always put on a bridle when standing on the nearside. Hold the top of the bridle in your right hand.

Left: Having approached the horse or pony, invite him to accept the bit by giving it to him with your left hand.

Right: After you have placed the bit into the horse's mouth, take the headcollar over the ears. Next you must check that the tongue of the horse is under the bit and that the bridle is in a correct position.

Right: Finally tighten the bridle, and check the space between the horse's head and throatlash by seeing that three fingers can be placed between them. The gap between the head and noseband must also be checked.

Snaffle

Double bridle

Pelham

The Weymouth bit combines a snaffle with a curb chain, attached to cheek rings. The curb pulls in the horse's head when appropriate pressure is applied on the reins. This bridle, when not used with care and consideration, can be quite severe on the horse.

The Pelham bridle combines the action of the snaffle and curb bit in one.

The Weymouth and Pelham bridles both have double reins. The top rein acts on the bit; the lower rein on the chain.

A leather headcollar or webbing halter are used for tying up a horse or for leading it.

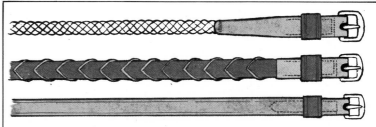

Above: Three types of ordinary reins. Top, a Dartnall rein made from cotton and sometimes from a man-made fibre; middle, a webbing rein with 'v' pieces of leather worked in; a plain leather rein, one of the most common now in use.

TYPES OF BIT

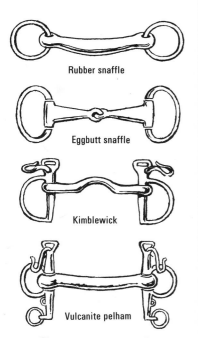

Rubber snaffle

Eggbutt snaffle

Kimblewick

Vulcanite pelham

Weymouth

THE LOOSE BOX

A loose box should be large enough to enable a horse to lie down easily without becoming cast. It must also be high enough to give sufficient headroom. To give maximum height at the door, a box should have its roof sloping away from the stable opening.

A loose box must be light and airy and, most important of all, it must be draught-proof. The positioning of the window will go a long way towards keeping draughts out. A window that is placed high up the wall may not necessarily avoid this problem of draught.

The fact that horses can and do stand up to the most severe weather conditions without seeming to suffer from the cold does not mean they are not susceptible to draughts.

A loose box must always be well ventilated, but never draughty.

Right: Before travelling, ensure the horse is fully protected. This rather special 'tacking-up' must be carried out before leaving for a show, and always before leaving the showground for the journey home.

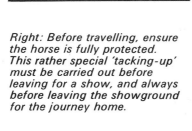

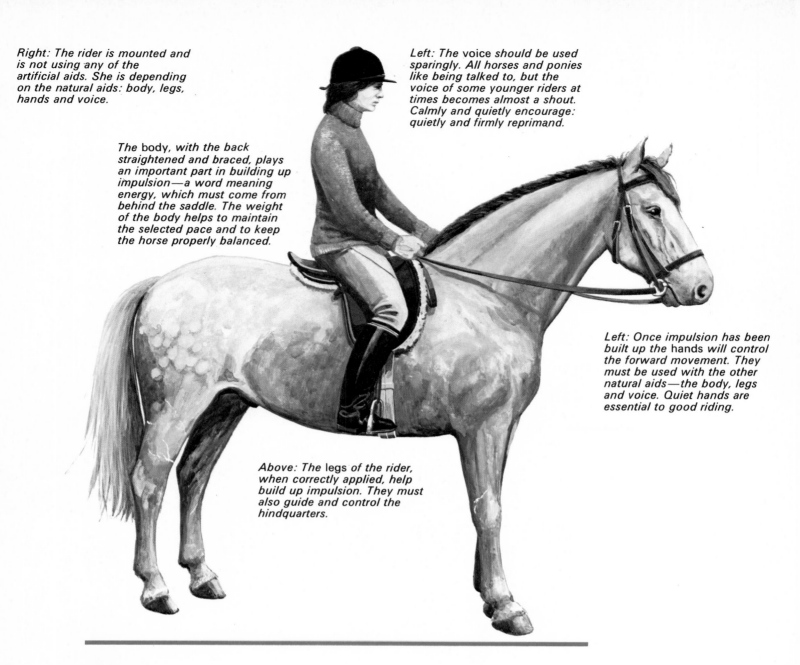

Right: The rider is mounted and is not using any of the artificial aids. She is depending on the natural aids: body, legs, hands and voice.

The body, with the back straightened and braced, plays an important part in building up impulsion—a word meaning energy, which must come from behind the saddle. The weight of the body helps to maintain the selected pace and to keep the horse properly balanced.

Left: The voice should be used sparingly. All horses and ponies like being talked to, but the voice of some younger riders at times becomes almost a shout. Calmly and quietly encourage: quietly and firmly reprimand.

Left: Once impulsion has been built up the hands will control the forward movement. They must be used with the other natural aids—the body, legs and voice. Quiet hands are essential to good riding.

Above: The legs of the rider, when correctly applied, help build up impulsion. They must also guide and control the hindquarters.

Learning to Ride

There are no short cuts when you are learning to ride. Riding demands an understanding of many basic points which have to be mastered before you can safely take a horse out. You will need many lessons and some of them will mean doing the same thing over and over again.

Lots of younger people, when starting to ride, find this a boring time. How wrong they are! All that is taught in the early stage will help throughout their riding life. To learn what is right, you must have patience. As your lessons become more complicated, you will find that you still have to think back to these early lessons. The most experienced horsemen will admit that, when they sense they are developing bad habits, they go right back to these early lessons.

Remember during these first lessons: be prepared to *learn, listen, watch* and *practise*. These four simple rules will lead you on your way to good and safe horsemanship, which will bring fun and enjoyment to you—and to your horse or pony.

The aids

The 'aids' are the signals used by the rider to tell his horse or pony what he should do.

There are two types of aids. The first are known as the *natural aids*. These are the signals passed to the horse by the rider by correct use of the body, legs, hands and voice. The second are *artificial aids*: stick, spurs and martingales.

It is best not to use the artificial aids when you are learning to ride. Younger riders, even on experienced ponies, will gain far more by learning how to apply the natural aids.

Aids should always be applied quietly and smoothly without undue fuss. A horse must be taught to recognize an aid when applied and to obey it immediately. But that will not happen if the signals are incorrectly given or applied. It takes practice for both horse and rider to achieve the best results, and aids wrongly given delay both from developing technique and skill.

For neatness as well as for safety most horses and ponies are turned-out to very high standards. But that cannot always be said of the riders!

Correct dress, which is not the same as expensive dress, should be worn at all times—even when in the stable yard or paddock.

There are four essential items of clothing for the rider: a hard riding hat; a pair of riding trousers or jodhpurs; a jacket or a long-sleeved sweater; and boots or shoes with heels, to prevent the feet from sliding through the stirrup irons.

The importance of a hard hat need hardly be emphasized. When riding, the strap should always be under the chin. Accidents so quickly happen, and prevention of accidents to the head are minimized by the wearing of the right head gear.

Trousers and jackets also have protective qualities. The importance of boots or shoes with heels need not be stressed to those who know how it feels to have their feet slide through the irons.

Above: Three very well turned-out riders being schooled under the watchful eye of their instructor.

At such instructional periods a watch is made on the position of the body, seat, legs and hands, and any faults will be corrected.

Below: A guide for measuring the length of leathers is to pull the stirrup and leathers out from the saddle until they reach under your armpit, then buckle.

Balance and Collection

All riders must understand the meaning of the words *balance* and *collection*, since both play a critical part in all movements of the horse. They must also understand that unless a horse or pony is properly balanced he can never be collected.

A horse is said to be balanced when his weight, and that of his rider, is spread evenly over each leg to enable him to use himself with ease and maximum efficiency. A horse running 'free', that is without a rider, is able to adjust his own balance. But this balance is quickly and easily upset once a rider takes up position. Balance is something all riders should learn to *feel*. Schooling and training help develop the muscles of the horse upon which good balance depends, and these muscles play an important role in all his movements.

A horse is collected when his energy (or impulsion) is concentrated so that his entire body shape is shortened. Young riders must remember that energy in a horse comes from behind the saddle; the hands of the rider should do no more than control the force thus built up. It is then, with active hindquarters and a relaxed mouth, that the horse has the best control of his limbs. Being collected also means that the horse is in a position to obey and act upon any aid given him by the rider.

Both balance and collection will be improved with schooling and training.

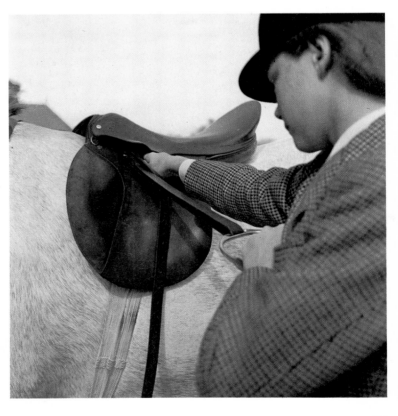

MOUNTING

Below: Stand with your shoulder against the horse's head.

Right: Hold the leather with your right hand and place your left foot into the stirrup.

Left: With your right hand take hold of the cantle and raise yourself from the ground.

Right: Swing up and over, taking care not to kick the horse as you do so!

Mounting

Horses and ponies do not always respond quickly to learning something new. But once they have been taught with patience and kindness they seldom forget. The early lessons teaching a horse to stand still at the halt are repaid over and over again when the time comes to mount or dismount.

The procedure for mounting is straighforward. First, check that the girth is tight so as to avoid the saddle slipping round when you take hold.

Stand with your left shoulder against the horse's head, holding the reins in your left hand. Take the near-side leather in your right hand and place your left foot into the stirrup.

Hold firmly to the reins, placing your right hand on the cantle of the saddle. Now swing your body up and, making sure the toes of your left foot are pointing downwards, throw your right leg over the horse's quarters. Lower yourself gently into the saddle and put your right foot into the stirrup. Sit well down, and take the reins in both hands. At this stage the leathers may require some adjustment, or the girth may need tightening.

Dismounting

To dismount you do not reverse the mounting procedure. Once you have come to a halt, remove both feet from the stirrups. Hold the reins once again quite firmly in the left hand and bring your right hand back to the cantle. Then, taking the body weight on to your arms (the left hand, with the reins, will be resting at the front of the saddle) swing your right leg over the quarters and vault to the ground, landing on your toes.

You will now be facing the near-side of the horse, still holding the reins in your left hand.

Having dismounted, run up the stirrup irons on both sides, return to the near-side and loosen the girth. Take the reins quietly over the horse's head and lead him back to his stable before unsaddling.

Below: Once mounted, check the girth and the length of your stirrup irons again. Lift the saddle flap as shown, and check the girth with your fingers. To adjust it, undo each buckle in turn, and pull the strap up, using your index finger to guide the buckle.

Right: A young rider photographed before a lesson. The hands of this young lady must not be criticized since she is trying to control her pony who is not at all happy to be facing the camera!

AT THE END OF A RIDE

After riding out, and when a few hundred metres from your stable yard, it is a good idea to dismount, run-up the leathers, slightly loosen the girth, and walk your horse or pony quietly back. This will enable him to relax and cool down. However, you must not permit him to be lazy. You, the rider, must lead him with a good stride (even though you may feel tired) and you must see your horse is alert and enjoying having you off his back! Walk facing oncoming traffic, keeping yourself between the traffic and the horse.

If you follow this procedure you will see why we emphasize the need to teach every horse to stand quite still when at the halt. It is one thing to dismount in the stable yard, when the horse knows he will be fed or allowed to run free and that the saddle and tack will be removed. It is quite another thing to dismount away from home and have a brisk, bright walk back to the yard.

DISMOUNTING

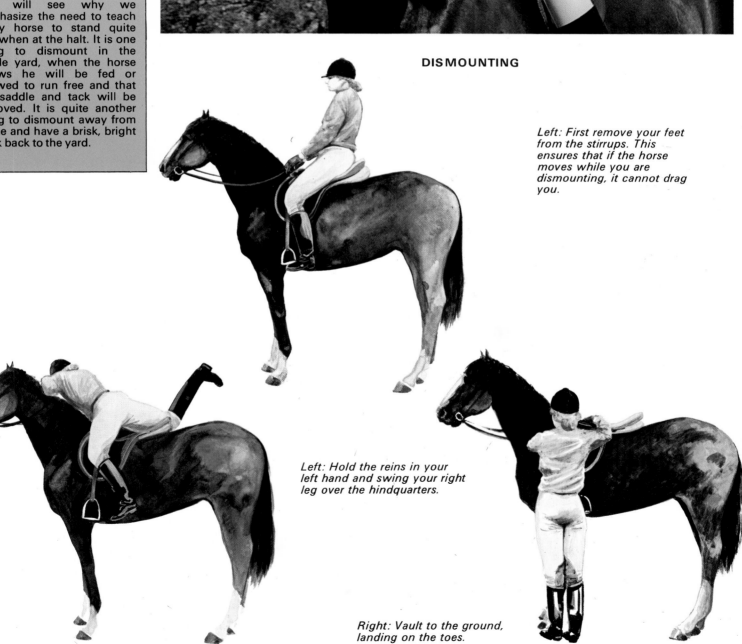

Left: First remove your feet from the stirrups. This ensures that if the horse moves while you are dismounting, it cannot drag you.

Left: Hold the reins in your left hand and swing your right leg over the hindquarters.

Right: Vault to the ground, landing on the toes.

The Paces

A horse or pony has four natural paces or gaits: walk, trot, canter and gallop. At a walk the pace should have four steps to the stride; at a trot this changes to two steps; at the canter to three steps; and at the gallop to four steps. These steps must be regular in their rhythm and maintained throughout each pace. Moving in any pace which is broken or irregular, or when the wrong foot is leading, is known as being 'disunited'. In addition to the four normal paces there are also collected, extended and free paces, shown below.

The halt, though not a pace, is an essential part of being able to move forward smoothly. The horse or pony should stand quite still, with his weight evenly distributed over all four legs. He should look attentive and be ready to move off immediately the instructions (aids) are given by the rider. A horse must stand still when the rider is mounting. It must not begin to move forward as soon as the rider's foot is in the stirrup!

Coming back to the halt is done progressively. For example, coming back to a halt from a canter means moving back to the trot and the walk before stopping.

Unless a rider understands the paces and until he or she knows how to move in and out of each, he cannot school or exercise his horse successfully. In fact, a rider should not ride out until he appreciates what all the paces mean and how they are achieved and maintained.

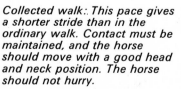

Above: The American Tennessee Walking Horse is a fine example of a horse bred for its gait.
Below: A horse being lunged at the canter.

Below, right: Mr Vin Toulson on Hunter's Moon showing the gallop at the Royal Show, Stoneleigh.

Collected walk: This pace gives a shorter stride than in the ordinary walk. Contact must be maintained, and the horse should move with a good head and neck position. The horse should not hurry.

Extended walk: Here the horse strides out, yet he must not be allowed to hurry his pace or lose the regular rhythm. The rider keeps contact at all times, but allows the horse to stretch his head and neck.

Free walk: The rider 'gives' fully to allow the horse freedom of his head and neck. The reins must be slack enough to permit easy movement, but the pace should be clearly marking the four beats of the walk.

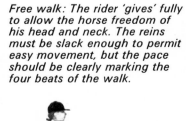

WALK

After mounting, check the girth and sit well down in the centre of the saddle. Keep your back straight but relaxed, and look ahead. The knees and thighs should be close to the saddle, with the lower parts of the legs free. Rest the balls of the feet

against the bars of the stirrups, with the heels lower than the toes. Apply and keep a light contact with the pony's mouth. To move forward, squeeze the lower parts of the legs against the pony's sides, slightly behind the girth. Maintain contact with

your hands and adjust your body weight. Next, slightly 'open' your hands, bringing the pony up to the bit, and move off. To bring your pony back to the halt, sit well into the saddle and straighten your spine. Close the lower part of

your legs and keep an even pressure. 'Close' the hands to bring the pony back to the bit. The pressure of your legs and the resistance felt through the bit brings the pony to a halt position. He should then stand quietly and square.

TROT

To move from a walk to a trot, increase pressure with the lower part of the legs. Shorten the reins to bring your pony well up to the bit. As he

responds, squeeze your legs to hold the pace. Next ease the reins but keep contact with the pony's mouth.
The two ways of riding at a

trot are the 'sitting' and 'rising' positions. The sitting trot is used when making the transition from the trot to another pace. In the rising trot,

keep a straight back and do not lean forward. Grip well with the thighs and knees. Your legs must remain quite still against the pony's sides.

CANTER

To move from the trot to the canter, increase pressure with both legs behind the girth. Sit well down in the saddle and keep the pony well up to the bit.

When cantering, keep close contact with the saddle. The pony should move into his stride with the foreleg leading. A pony is cantering 'disunited' or 'false' when, in moving to

the left, the off-fore leads or, to the right, the near-fore leads. The incorrect use of the rider's body weight easily upsets the pace of a canter. Do not lean too far forward or you may lose

full control and the pony will tend to move on too quickly and unevenly. The canter is the most difficult pace to perform well and both pony and rider need plenty of practice.

The gallop is a pace seldom used by the younger rider. In this pace the rider adopts a forward position, with his weight as near as possible to the centre of gravity. The

rider's body weight should be taken on the knees and stirrups. At all times the rider must be in control. Never let the horse take over. There is nothing worse than seeing a rider galloping on

when it is obvious that he is being taken at this pace. When the going is good or when riding over sands, a gallop can be enjoyed by both pony and rider.

At all four paces it is essential that the rider, by using the correct aids, keeps control and is able to move through the paces and back to the halt without undue stress on the pony.

GALLOP

Schooling and Exercising

Left: Lungeing should not be carried out by the inexperienced. Watch a lungeing session by a qualified trainer, but do not attempt to copy this without an older, experienced person with you. The object of lungeing is to teach quietness and obedience; to encourage a forward movement; to help develop the muscles on both flanks of the horse or pony, and to improve balance. A horse being lunged on a left-hand circle will require the trainer to hold the lunge rein in the left hand and to use the lungeing whip in the right hand. These positions are reversed when lungeing to the right.

Below: One of the first steps in teaching a horse or pony to jump is to ask him to walk and trot over poles laid on the ground. This will teach the horse to stretch as he moves through the line, and the rider will develop confidence. The distance between poles will vary slightly according to the stride of the horse. Try a distance of 1·5 metres (5 ft) between each of the poles, and make adjustments from there.

A horse or pony at grass will take exercise as and when he feels like it. Frequently, for no apparent reason, he will suddenly stop grazing and set off for a quick canter and possibly a buck or two, and then, almost as suddenly, stop and resume grazing. This is the natural form of exercise that animals take, but if it went unchecked you would have a horse that is hard to catch and harder still to ride!

During schooling and exercising periods the object is to teach an immediate obedience to all the aids correctly given; the development of suppleness; and the build-up of muscles. To this end, schooling and exercising should be carried out according to a planned programme. Consider what you intend to achieve over, say, a two-month period and then set about this in a calm and orderly fashion.

The Schooling area

If you have no schooling area (or manége), mark out a piece of level ground of about 40 by 20 metres. This is the ideal space in which to practise circles, turns, serpentines, figures-of-eight and so on.

To achieve the obedience required when schooling, it is necessary for both rider and horse to be able to concentrate on the work in hand. It is far better to school in a quiet corner of a field than in a well-planned manége laid out in an area where distractions, such as other horses or a busy road, will take away concentration.

Right: After you have taken your horse or pony over poles laid on the ground, and had a practice session with the cavalletti, move on to a small built obstacle. This is better than going straight into practice jumps.

The picture shows how a young horse is asked to jump a combination of low-built fences. Provided the distance between the fences is right (see page 43), and provided the rider has built up sufficient impulsion and encourages the horse to jump 'through' the two elements, there should be no problem.

One of the problems which arises when schooling a horse is how to avoid repetition. Horses become bored when the same exercise is repeated again and again. So you must learn how far you should go along one routine before asking the horse to rest or try another exercise. A short lesson is frequently more productive than a long, tedious session of going over the same thing time after time. For example, do not keep going for too long on one rein. Horses must be able to adjust quickly to changes of rein.

But schooling or exercising need not be confined to the riding school or manège. Use every opportunity you have, even when out hacking. Make your pony halt, and then lead him quietly through the paces to the canter. Keep the canter going for a while and then bring him back to the halt. Teach him to stand still and square and not to move until you apply the aids asking him to move off. A horse who fidgets at the halt can be very difficult even in the stable yard. There is nothing better than having a pony who will stand still while being tacked up and mounted. And how important it is that he should stand quite still when you arrive back home and have to dismount!

The experience and skill of the rider is critical to the development of the horse, and it will not be easy for an inexperienced rider to use schooling time to the best advantage. This is one of the many reasons why younger riders should have continual riding instruction.

Right: Cavalletti are perhaps the most useful of all practice fences. They are very adaptable —by turning a cavalletto over, the height can be raised or lowered. From the picture you will see that the pole on the front cavalletto is on the top of the cross-piece. This would give a height of 48cm (19 inches.). Moving it over the height will come down to 38cm (15 inches), and when the pole is under the fence the height will be 25 cm (10 inches).

4. Landing

3. Suspension

2. Taking off

Jumping Technique

There are few riders of any age who do not relish the thrill of jumping.

Once work on the 'flat' has reached a satisfactory standard, and the horse is obedient to the aids and the rider has mastered, even in basic terms, the value of collection and impulsion, the time has come to begin jumping.

The building-up of impulsion, and the balance of horse and rider certainly play their part in jumping, but it is the rider's position at the moment of take-off which really matters.

The rider should keep his head up and look ahead in the direction he is going. Do not look down, for the slightest movement of the rider during the actual jump can upset balance and the horse's concentration. The body should be as still as possible and the back straight and supple. The shoulders should be very slightly forward.

The arms, bent at the elbows, must be kept close to the rider's sides and be able to follow the movement of the horse's head and 'give' as he reaches out to jump. The legs, too, are important. They should be used to maintain impulsion, the lower part of each leg remaining close to the horse's sides. The legs should not 'flap'. When jumping you should use shorter leathers than when hacking or schooling.

As the horse arrives at the point of take-off, the rider should not be out of the saddle. He should remain close to it, ensuring that impulsion is maintained. As the horse takes off, he will stretch his neck and the rider's hands must follow. Never sit back at this moment and pull back with your hands. This will act as a check, and the horse will not know whether he should stop or go on.

During the period of suspension, the rider will follow the movements of the horse and, on landing, he must not bounce back into the saddle.

The horse should be kept in the rider's control during the entire process of jumping. On landing, the horse should still be 'on the bit', that is you should have maintained contact with the mouth. Both rider and horse should have recovered after two or three strides and able to move off to the next obstacle.

It is important that the technique of jumping should be learned and developed through good instruction. It is not easy to *know* what you may be doing wrong when you are seated on your horse. But much can be seen from the ground and it is from here where good advice can be given.

Left: Jumping clear at a water jump at a major show.

Left: The sequence shows a horse in the act of approaching and jumping a spread fence. Note the rider's excellent jumping position. Her balance is good throughout, and her hands have allowed the horse to move over and through the fence without any difficulty.

Right and below: Four types of fences found in most novice and junior show jumping courses. Top: a rustic gate. Centre, right: a rustic fence with a brush to give it some filling. Below: a combination of upright jumps. Below, right: a parallel of green and white poles.

1. The approach

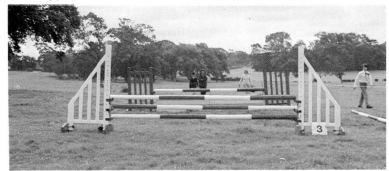

Below: A young rider jumping a 'natural' fence in a hunter trial.

About Show Jumping

Of all the equestrian sports perhaps show jumping is the most popular for both competitors and spectators. Television has brought the thrill and precision of jumping into millions of homes, and the major national and international competitions, whether held in indoor arenas or in the vast open areas such as Aachen or Hickstead, attract enormous crowds.

The standard of show jumping varies considerably from show to show. All who learn to ride can hardly wait to jump. And even the beginners are catered for in competitions where the highest fence on the course is perhaps set at 38cm (15 inches)!

Show jumping brings all ages and all types of horses and ponies into competition. The courses set are designed for the conditions prevailing, just as the nature of the obstacles are planned for the level or grading of those taking part.

The length of the course and the number of fences to be jumped will seldom be the same. It may be this which makes show jumping such an absorbing sport.

Other than 'speed' competitions, show jumping competitions usually end with a jump-off. In speed competitions the fastest time and lowest number of faults, or the fastest time with faults penalized as an extension of time, will produce a result.

A jump-off 'against the clock' will take place only where there has been equality of faults in the first rounds. It is then that the fastest time, and the lowest number of faults, decides the winner.

Right: This diagram shows the type of course with ten obstacles that might be set for a novice class.

Having gone through the start, fence 1 will be an inviting spread fence asking and encouraging the horse to go on. Fence 2 is an upright; 3 an ascending spread; 4 a gate; 5 a combination comprising an upright into an ascending oxer; 6 an upright of poles; 7 another combination, this time a parallel into an upright; fence 8 a gate; 9 a spread, and 10 a wall. Then straight ahead and through the finish.

Below: Harvey Smith, one of the world's top-class riders, shows how simple it is to jump a wall! Note the position of Harvey's head and observe that his eyes are already on the next obstacle.

Below right: Competitors, officials and spectators stand and salute as national anthems are played before the start of the main event at the world-renowned Aachen showground in Germany.

Bottom, right: Showing two pairs of clean heels!

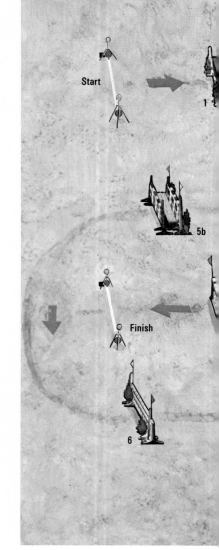

2   3

5a

4

9

8

7a   7b

TRUE DISTANCES

The so-called 'true' distances which should be set on flat ground for a combination made up of one non-jumping stride are listed below. Where the 'going' is downhill allow for the lengthening of a horse's stride by 30cm (12ins). An Uphill approach will mean a shortening of between 15 and 25cm.

Upright to upright:
Horses: 8 metres (26ft)
Ponies: 6·85 metres (22ft 6ins)

Upright to parallel:
Horses: 7·60 metres (25ft)
Ponies: 6·55 metres (21ft 6ins)

Upright to ascending oxer:
Horses: 7·50 metres (24ft 6ins)
Ponies: 6·40 metres (21ft)

Ascending oxer to upright:
Horses: 8 metres (26ft)
Ponies: 6·85 metres (22ft 6ins)

Parallel to upright:
Horses: 7·85 metres (25ft 6ins)
Ponies: 6·70 metres (22ft)

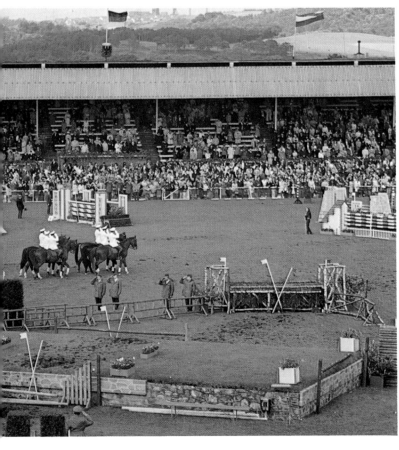

The cross-country course demands a horse and rider that are both courageous and fit enough to stand up to jumping fixed obstacles and water at the speed demanded by the competition.

The dressage phase requires complete obedience of the horse as it responds to the aids given by the rider.

After other events, the horse must complete the show jumping phase which requires precision and skill.

Combined Training

Horse trials are sometimes known as Eventing or Combined Training. These competitions include three separate tests: dressage, cross country and show jumping. The tests are judged separately, and the marks awarded at each stage are used cumulatively to determine the result.

Interest in Eventing and Horse Trials is world wide. Owners dream of having horses and ponies sufficiently fit, supple, obedient and courageous to undertake this type of competition. They know the patience, skill and training that is necessary for success.

The levels of Events fall into three categories: Championship, Standard, Novice and Junior. Championship and International Three-Day Events, as with official Standard and Novice Events, are conducted and judged under the Rules established by the Fédération Equestre Internationale (FEI). These rules are at times modified by the various national bodies. For example, in Britain the Combined Training Committee of the British Horse Society guides and controls the sport.

Where an Event is not staged by the official body, the rules and conditions will be shown on the published schedules. And these must be examined most closely before you enter a competition! Younger riders are well served at events organized under Pony Club guidance.

The Three Main Types of Horse Trial
The One-day event: The three tests take place during the day and the result is declared before the competitors leave.
The Two-day event: This starts with a dressage competition, followed by a cross-country test, including a steeplechase. The show jumping phase is on the second day.
The Three-day event: This is the most exacting of all riding competitions with each of the tests taking place on successive days.

Dressage

The word 'dressage' in French means schooling or training. In equitation this implies a rather special type of schooling which ultimately covers *haute école,* or high school, a level of near perfect co-operation between horse and rider.

In the dressage arena, the tests are set out to show the standard of obedience and suppleness of the horse. The animal undertakes, without any obvious or flamboyant movements, a test to show how well it has been schooled to obey the slightest demand of the rider. The dressage test includes a series of circles, serpentines, turns, lateral movements, passes and half-passes. The horse will be asked to show changes of leg and pace and to follow the patterns laid down with calmness and balance.

The judge in a dressage competition will award marks on each animal's performance (10 for perfection down to 1 for very bad). He or she will also comment on the score sheet and these comments are given to the owner or rider.

Marks are awarded for smoothness of action, accuracy in carrying out the test, lightness of touch, impulsion, and the immediate response of the horse to the aids given by the rider. The overall picture and the balance achieved throughout the test are also taken into account. When carried out to perfection, it appears that the horse is moving through the test with no assistance from the rider.

Below: A score sheet showing how a judge might mark a Test at novice standard. The first column shows the number of the part of the Test. The second, the letters as shown on the arena plan (right). The third column explains the particular test. The fourth gives the maximum possible marks, and the fifth the marks awarded. Finally, at each stage of the Test the judge notes some comment.

Above: The movements in a dressage test are based on the gaits, turns, halt and rein-back of everyday riding. Each test is conducted at a marked position in the arena. These positions are shown by letters, and the horse and rider perform at and between the letters to an agreed programme. This horse is showing a few lengthened strides.

The dressage tests are a display of discipline and control. This is shown in the careful dress of the rider and the appearance of the horse as well as in their performance in the ring.

Below: This plan shows the markings of a dressage arena of normal dimensions. At international level the size of the arena is increased from 20×40 metres to 20×60 metres. All tests, of whatever standard, are designed to make use of the entire area of the arena.

		The scale of marks is as follows:
10. Excellent	5. Sufficient	
9. Very good	4. Insufficient	
8. Good	3. Fairly bad	
7. Fairly good	2. Bad	
6. Satisfactory	1. Very bad	
	0. Not performed	

THE BRITISH HORSE SOCIETY'S

DRESSAGE TEST

NUMBER 12

(Novice standard) 1974

Approximate Time – 4½ mins

Errors over the course are penalised:

First Error	2 marks
Second Error	4 marks
Third Error	8 marks
Fourth Error	Elimination

No. .... HORSE .... RIDER ....

		Test	Max. Marks 1	Judge's Marks 1 to 10 2	Observations
1.	A X	Enter at working trot (sitting) Halt. Salute. Proceed at working trot (rising)	10	7	Straight entry. Quarters a little to left in halt. Smooth move off.
2.	C	Track right	10	6	More activity needed.
3.	A	Working trot (sitting) serpentine 3 loops, each loop to go to the side of the arena finishing at C	10	6	Coming above bit at times. Well shaped loops.
4.	M B BAE	Working canter right Circle right 20m diameter Working canter	10	8	Smooth strike off. Good Circle.
5.	Between E&H K	Half circle right 15m diameter returning to the track between F&K Working trot (sitting)	10	4	Hollowing and becoming unbalanced before K. Trotted too soon.
6.	A C	Working trot (rising) serpentine 3 loops each loop to go to the side of the arena finishing at C Working trot (sitting)	10	6	Hollow in first loop, improving. Last loop good.
7.	H, E EAB	Working canter left Circle left 20m diameter Working canter	10	7	Hind legs need to come underneath a little more.
8.	Between B&M F	Half circle left 15m diameter returning to the track between B&F Working trot (sitting)	10	7	Much better half circle. Canter well maintained.
9.	A KXM	Working trot (rising) Change rein and show a few lengthened strides	10	5	Hurried more than lengthened.
10.	C HXF	Medium walk Change rein at a free walk on a long rein	10	8	Good active free walk.
11.	F A G	Working trot (sitting) Down centre line Halt. Salute. Leave arena at walk on a long rein at A	10	6	Straight down centre, but some resistance in mouth to halt.
12.		General impression, obedience and calmness	10	6	Not always round enough. Hind legs need bringing more underneath horse.
13.		Paces and impulsion	10	7	Smooth paces, needing a little more activity. Good walk.
14.		Position and seat of the rider and correct application of the aids	10	6	Fairly good position, but inclined to lean inwards on right rein.
		TOTAL	140	89	

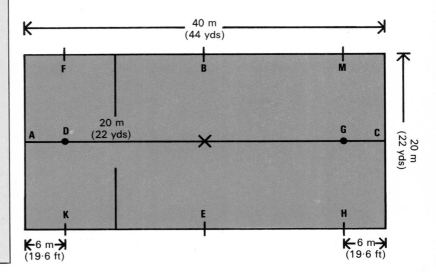

Left: Miss Virginia Holgate and Dubonnet jumping the Normandy Bank at the Badminton Horse Trials.

Cross Country Phase and Hunter Trials

The object of the second phase of the one-, two- or three-day Event is to prove that the horse has speed, endurance and the ability to jump fixed obstacles and water hazards when being ridden across country. It also tests the skill and judgement of the rider when riding at selected speeds and paces.

Separate from Eventing are those competitions called 'Hunter Trials'. In these competitions there is no dressage or show jumping phase. The object is to plan a day when all competitors can jump a cross-country course. The obstacles should be natural-looking and of a 'fixed' nature.

Most organizers of Hunter Trials design their schedules to include classes suited to riders and horses with varying degrees of experience and ability. There will almost certainly be a class for novices; an 'open' competition in which all may enter; a class for those living within a set distance of the site of the trials, and perhaps a class for juniors.

The rules laid down by the FEI still apply to a degree in Hunter Trials. The course is measured, and a time is worked out based on the horse maintaining a speed of so many yards or metres a minute. Time penalties are incurred by riders who take longer than the time allowed. And these penalties are added to any other penalties gathered on the way round, by refusals, falls or for other reasons!

Eventing, therefore, should not be confused with Hunter Trials. There can be little doubt that Eventing at any level is the most exacting of all equestrian sports. What a thrill it is to have a horse that can maintain the quiet control and discipline of the dressage phase; the courage and determination to complete the cross country phase; and the precision demanded by the final show jumping section.

Right: In Horse Trials it is quite commonplace throughout the world to find many competitors from all ranks of the army, air force and navy.

One of the more natural obstacles on a course would be a hedge or a gate. Specially constructed fences, as some of the pictures on these pages show, are devised to appear as natural as possible. Their design and structure will depend on the ground and type of terrain being covered by the Event.

Above: Into the water splash, a traditional obstacle in cross-country riding.

Right: A very firmly 'fixed' natural obstacle well cleared by competitor number 132.

Below right: Jumping cleanly over one of the many different obstacles facing the Eventer. The car to the left will probably belong to the judge appointed to this obstacle.

47

The Show Scene

What is it that makes up a showing class? In the showing rings we might expect to find classes for a Leading Rein pony; a Child's First pony; a Child's Ridden pony; a Working Hunter pony; Novice ponies of many types (usually judged according to height); Hack and Cob classes; Side-saddle events; separate Breed classes; classes for different groupings of Mountain and Moorland ponies; Arab and Anglo-Arab classes; and the range of Hunter classes bringing in the Lightweight, Middleweight and Heavyweight hunters who are in part judged according to their ability and capability of carrying different weights. There are also classes in the showing ring for judging the rider's ability and skill.

And then, for those who enjoy showing, the ultimate: the showing and judging of the horse or pony to stand as champion or reserve champion of his class.

American classes

In American shows there are in addition a wonderfully inventive range of specialized classes covering those who ride for fun to those who produce for the judges horses with both skill and manners to undertake the most exacting of 'shows'. There will also be Parade classes in which the riders are mounted on elaborately made saddles, with all the other equipment and bridles created in the most exotic designs. There are also Western classes and a host of other events planned to show the horse to the best advantage. In Australia, New Zealand, South Africa and many countries of Europe, the showing scene is rather like that in Britain.

Above: The first competitions facing most younger riders are those on the leading rein. This rider and pony, together with the young lady holding the leading rein, look confident and are well turned-out.

Below: Shetland ponies—the smallest of the British native pony breeds.

Right: These two gentlemen, prizewinners in a Hunter class, show clearly the high standard of turn-out required for both horse and rider when showing. The fine horses are groomed to perfection and well tacked-up. The riders are dressed to complement their mounts.

Right: Judging conformation is part of the working hunter pony classes.

Right: A beautifully presented horse and cart in one of the display classes now becoming so popular at many shows throughout the world. Take particular note of the equipment of the horse and the way the driver has complete control.

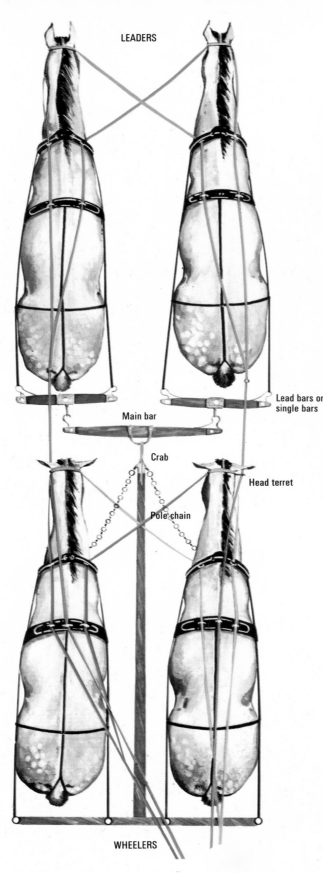

LEADERS

Lead bars or
single bars

Main bar

Crab

Pole chain

Head terret

WHEELERS

How to hold the reins of
a four-in hand

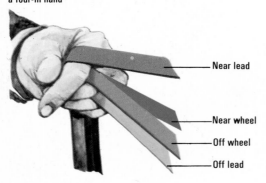

Near lead

Near wheel

Off wheel

Off lead

Driving

Imagine what it must be like seated high above a team of four horses and knowing they will be controlled by the reins held in your left hand!

To make clearer which rein is which we have asked our artist to colour each rein differently. The picture at the foot of the page gives a key so that the reader can follow the reins through to the bits on each of the four horses.

The pair in front are called the 'leaders'; the pair nearest the coach are the 'wheelers'.

Moving off is quite a complicated procedure. The wheelers, who must be ready for the signal 'Walk on', move first. This pair is also involved in the stopping of a coach (should it be necessary) when it is going downhill.

When turning on either rein the leaders will begin their movement when the coachman adjusts the reins and gives the aid. But, at this time, it would prove disastrous were the wheeler to begin to turn. They must be restrained, and this is but one small part of the skill the coachman shows in handling the reins.

Driving, as the pictures on these pages show, involves a number of different types of coaches and carriages. It has, during recent years, become a major international sport. It is one which demands great skill, enormous patience, a love of horses, and the ability to control one horse or a team in all circumstances.

Above: The Hon Mrs J Kidd, with her well-known pair of ponies, Maple Brantly and Maple Augusta, at Hickstead, Sussex.

Top right: A dashing team of four horses being driven in competition. Note the traditional harness with bells attached. The driver needs enormous skill to take his team round the arena at this speed.

Right: A handsome pair of horses being shown to the judges in a Driving class.

Below: Owners of racehorses each have their individual colours which are worn by the jockey on his cap and shirt. These colours are known as 'silks'.

The Racing Scene

Not until Charles II came to the British throne in 1660 was bloodstock breeding of racehorses taken really seriously. Later three Arab stallions were brought to Britain: the now famed Byerley Turk, Darley Arabian and Godolphin Arabian. These three Arab stallions were mated with the best of the British mares and from these lines came the Thoroughbred— surely supreme as a racehorse!

In 1752 the Jockey Club meeting at Newmarket decided on a number of rules of racing and the sport became organized. The first of the classic races, the St Leger, was run in 1776, and the first of the handicap races followed shortly afterwards with a race at Ascot in 1791. From that date to the present we have much to be grateful to the Jockey Club for, since the rules of racing as laid down by them have been accepted throughout the world.

red and yellow halved, sleeves reversed

green with brown hoop

black and yellow quartered

maroon and blue stripes, blue sleeves

brown with white sash and sleeves

Left: 'They're off!' That shout is heard as the starters leave the stalls. Before being put into the starting stalls, the horses will have been paraded in the paddock. The jockeys then mount up after the owner and trainer have had a final word about the race ahead. Only in flat races are the starting stalls used; in steeplechasing and hurdling the starter will raise the tape once the horses have approached in a straight line.

Left and right: The distances raced on the flat vary between five furlongs and eleven furlongs (a furlong is one-eighth of a mile). Most races are 'handicapped' races, which means that the better horses carry greater weights and thus make the chances of all runners equal. A weight for age scale is also in use and is the basis for modern handicapping.

THE GREAT RACES
The 'Triple Crown' of racing in Britain consists of the Derby, the Two Thousand Guineas and the St Leger.

The Triple Crown of the USA consists of the Kentucky Derby, the Preakness Stakes and the Belmont Stakes.

In France famous races include the Prix de l'Arc de Triomphe and the Grand Steeplechase de Paris.

Other famous races are the Melbourne Cup of Australia, the Irish Sweeps Derby and the Oaks, the Ascot Gold Cup and the greatest steeplechase of all—the Grand National.

The picture above, right, shows the runners at Tattenham Corner during the Derby, held at Epsom, Surrey.

Right: Harness racing, now growing in popularity throughout the world, includes racing known in some countries as trotting or pacing. Horses used in harness racing are bred for speed. They must also have stamina, since they have to draw a lightweight gig around tracks which are either lefthand or righthand circuits.

Right: Steeplechasing is probably the most exciting of all forms of racing. The word was derived from riders who raced each other across fields in Ireland, setting their course between one church steeple and another.
The fences look formidable, and, like hurdling, there are limits set to the number of obstacles in each mile. In steeplechasing the number is set at twelve fences in the first two miles, and six in each additional mile. Here, Spanish Steps leads Kilmore Boy and Red Rum over the first fence of the 1975 Grand National.

Left: Hurdle racing began in the early part of the nineteenth century and is held over distances of not less than two miles. The height of the hurdle is 1·2 m (3 ft 6 in), and there will not be more than four hurdles in each mile raced. This form of racing is very much part of the British and Irish scene but has not yet proved popular in Europe or the United States.

1 ▲

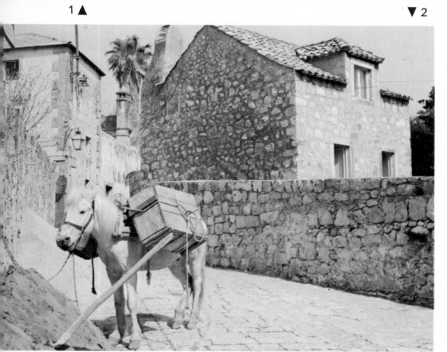

▼ 2

▼ 3

Horses at Work

In 1835 there were nearly 4000 mail and stage coaches on the roads of Britain. They used more than 15,000 horses and gave employment to 30,000 men. In 1918 there were more than a million horses still at work on the farms of Britain. Forty years later there were only about 50,000. The horse could now no longer be regarded mainly as a working animal.

Man's use of the horse has changed since he first hunted it for its meat, then, more than 5000 years ago, began to ride it. Its main use was as a beast of burden and for war or sport. Horses pulled chariots, carried soldiers into battle, carried hunters, raced or played a form of polo.

The heavily armoured knights of the Middle Ages needed powerful horses to carry them. So such horses were bred. It was from these European 'great' horses that the heavy draught horse is descended. Later, lighter, swifter steeds were needed in battle and the Arab was brought to Europe by the Crusaders. Thus man bred different horses to suit his various purposes.

Although horses were always kept as beasts of burden, to pull carts and carry heavy loads, it was not until the eighteenth century that they were widely used as farm animals in preference to oxen.

Even today, despite the internal combustion engine, which has largely replaced the horse on the roads and farms, horses can still be seen in many major towns and cities pulling loads through the busy streets, and be found working on farms, particularly where heavy soil makes it difficult to manoeuvre a tractor. They are still used too to manage cattle and sheep where they are grazed on the open range.

The military use of the horse is now almost entirely for ceremonial purposes. But horses continue to be used by the police for crowd control.

1 Horses are used to herd stock on the plains of North and South America. In Australia too they work with sheep and cattle. Here a stockman is collecting a calf. The cowboy or stockman depends as much on the skill and intelligence of his horse as the shepherd does upon his sheepdog.

2 From earliest times horses and ponies have been used as beasts of burden. This German pack pony has a large box container strapped to either side of a saddle so that it may carry a heavy load.

3 Mounted police, like this policewoman outside Buckingham Palace in London, are used to help with crowd control. The policewoman is seated high above the heads of pedestrians on a specially trained horse. From her position she can see to supervise the movements of the crowd.

4 In many countries of the world horses are still used to pull freight and passengers. This horse-drawn gharry works as a taxi in the busy streets of New Delhi in India.

5 At one time a horse was the most important possession of any farmer. In 1910 there were 20 million horses on the farms of America. Sixty years later there were reckoned to be only 7 million in the country. Yet today horses are still used to plough heavy soil in which tractors get bogged down or to work small farms which do not need expensive machinery.

6 Horses used to haul every type of commercial and private vehicle. During the First World War a Corps of Women Drivers was formed to man the mail vans.

▼4   5▲   ▼6

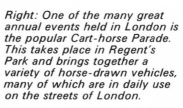

Left: One of the world-famous Lipizzaner stallions performing at the Spanish Riding School in Vienna. The School was founded during the sixteenth century and is the oldest riding academy in the world.

Right: One of the many great annual events held in London is the popular Cart-horse Parade. This takes place in Regent's Park and brings together a variety of horse-drawn vehicles, many of which are in daily use on the streets of London.

Far right: For centuries, horses have performed in the circus. One of the best known of these is the Crown Circus of Munich, at which the picture was photographed.

Left: Corporal Hurman of the Life Guards on Cicero, one of the most famous and best-loved of all military horses. Cicero has even had a film made about him and his work as a drum horse.

Right: Jousting is now presented as a display at many horse shows. Originally a joust was a combat between two knights or men-at-arms on horseback who opposed each other with lances.

Right: The rodeo dates back to the early part of the nineteenth century, when cowboys had learned the tricks needed to herd horses in the wild. The first recorded rodeo, as a public spectacle, took place in Colorado in 1869. Today, hundreds of rodeos take place throughout North America.

Above: Hunting is a traditional and popular winter sport. Co-operative farmers and landowners permit hunts to cross their land, and everything possible is done by the hunt and its followers to ensure no undue damage is done. Hunting obeys a number of strict rules. It is essential that those who hunt observe these at all times.

The picture above shows some of the Cottesmore Hunt crossing into a field near Oakham.

Below: Foxhounds await the call to move.

Horses and Sport

Most equestrian sports were developed for a purpose: fox hunting to rid farmers of their enemy the fox; polo to give practice to mounted warriors in the essential movements of horse and rider in battle.

Just as racehorses are especially bred, so these sports demand suitable horses, bred and trained to excel. Polo ponies are small, swift and lively; trained to turn and twist with the action of the game. Hunters are chosen for their stamina and intelligence and their ability to go well across the sort of country they are to be asked to hunt over. It is often from this hunter stock that the great show jumpers also come.

But to most horse owners simply riding out is their main sport, enjoying the pleasure of working together as a team.

Right: Pony trekking is a splendid way to enjoy a riding holiday, whether you are an experienced rider or are just beginning to learn to ride. In most cases trekking starts from a riding centre and returns a few hours later. The more experienced and venturesome may decide to go trailing where the ride extends over several days, finally returning to the starting point.

Right: The beginnings of polo are lost in time, though records exist of games played in 525 BC. Some have said the game originated in China, but it is most likely the game as we now know it began in Persia (Iran). The game was brought to England in 1869, and was introduced to America in about 1884.

The polo ground is 274 metres (300 yards) long and 146 metres (160 yards) wide. The game is made up of six chukkas, each lasting 7 minutes. At the end of each chukka a bell is rung but the game goes on until the ball goes out of play or the umpires call for a stop. Between each chukka there is an interval of 3 minutes; five minutes being allowed at half-time.

Glossary

AGED A horse that is seven years old or more.

AGEING The methods of telling the age of a horse by its teeth.

AIDS The signals given to a horse by a rider to convey his instructions. The *natural* aids are the rider's body, legs, hands and voice. The *artificial* aids are whips, spurs and martingales.

BANDAGES Protective strips of material, cotton, flannel or stockinette, used on the legs and tail.

BEDDING May be of straw, sawdust, wood shavings or peat.

BED DOWN The process of making a bed for a horse.

BEHIND THE BIT When a horse refuses to take a correct hold of the bit.

BLOOD HORSE The name given to the English Thoroughbred.

BRAIDING The American word for Plaiting (q.v.).

BRIDOON Known also as Bradoon. A small snaffle bit used in Double or Weymouth bridles.

BROOD MARE The name given to a mare used for breeding.

BRUSHING This takes place when a horse strikes the fore or hind leg with the one opposite. It results in cutting near the joints of a fetlock. Sometimes this is caused by bad action or conformation.

BRUSHING BOOTS Wide straps which give protection to the joints. Made from leather or felt with a padded protection. (See page 42.)

CAST (a) when a horse loses a shoe, (b) when a horse lies down in his box and is unable to get up. The most common reason for a horse to be cast is when the box is too small. or because he is lying too near a wall or other obstruction.

CLENCH The ends of the nails which are holding the shoe to the hoof. Clenches (sometimes the word clinch is used) are closed by the farrier hammering the end over and into the wall of the foot.

CLIPPING In winter, horses grow a thick coat. If they are ridden hard, they sweat and lose condition. Clipping (the cutting away of coat and mane) is then advisable. This can be done by hand or machine.

COLIC Any form of abdominal pain in a horse, usually caused by digestive trouble. Treatment of slight attacks can be given at home, but the vet should be called if colic is still apparent after half-an-hour.

COLLECTING RING The area adjacent to the showing ring where horses are collected

before entering for a competition.

COLT A young male up to four years of age.

COMBINATION Obstacles or fences in show jumping made up from two or three separate jumps and where the maximum distance between the first and the last must not exceed 12 metres (39ft 4ins). There are four categories or shapes of show jumping obstacles or fences: upright or vertical (1); parallel or square oxer (2); ascending oxer (3); and triple bar or staircase (4). Also illustrated is a hog's back (5), a shape which does not come under the four most commonly found types.

CONDITION A term used to denote the health and looks of a horse.

CRIB BITING Gripping the manger (crib) or door with the incisor teeth. If often produces wind-sucking which leads to indigestion.

CROSS-BREEDING When horses of different breeds are mated.

CURB-CHAIN A chain fitted to the curb or Pelham which must lie flat in the groove of the horse's jaw just above the lower lip.

DAM The female parent of a foal.

DISOBEDIENCE A word used in jumping and cross-country to denote refusals, circles, resistances, a run-out, stopping, napping and other disobedient acts, all of which are subject to penalties as detailed by the rules.

ELECTUARY A medical term used when drugs are made into a paste which has a base of treacle or honey.

FÉDÉRATION EQUESTRE INTERNATIONALE (FEI) The international governing body of equestrian sport.

FILLY A female horse under the age of four years.

FOAL A colt, gelding or filly, up to the age of twelve months. A male is a colt-foal; a female a filly-foal.

FODDER Sometimes the word forage is used. Both words describe any feeding stuffs fed to horses.

GALL A sore place caused by ill-fitting saddlery. A gall is usually found under the girth or saddle.

GELDING A castrated male horse of any age.

GOING A term which indicates the nature of the ground. It applies to the ground used for show jumping, racing or hunting. One will hear the words 'good going', 'soft going' or 'heavy going', each of which is self-explanatory.

HACKAMORE The best-known of the bitless bridles. It acts on the nose and chin but is not advised for novice riders since it can be most severe to the horse.

HALTER A webbing headcollar used for tying up a horse or for leading. See HEADCOLLAR.

HAND The term used for measuring the height of a horse. The word is derived from the width of a man's hand, now an agreed 10cm (4ins).

KNEE-CAPS A felt covering for the knees. They are normally reinforced with leather and are a protective device to use when travelling or exercising on hard going.

LAMINITIS Inflammation or fever of the feet caused by fast work on hard ground or too much heating food and insufficient exercise.

MARE A female horse or pony which has reached the age of four years.

MARTINGALE A device to regulate the horse's head carriage. It is a strap attached at one end to the noseband, reins or bit, and at the other to the girth.

NEW ZEALAND RUG A weatherproof rug made from canvas used on horses turned out in winter months.

NIGHT RUG A rug, sometimes fully lined, used to keep horses warm at night.

NUMNAH A sheepskin, felt, nylon or rubber pad which fits under a saddle.

OVER-FACED When a horse is being asked to jump obstacles which are beyond his capabilities.

OVER-REACH BOOTS A circular

rubber boot fitted to prevent injury to the coronet when a horse over-reaches.

OVER-REACHING The edge of the hind shoe striking against the coronet of the fore-foot.

PLAITING The process of making plaits to smarten the neck and general appearance before entering competitions. In most Showing classes all horses or ponies will be plaited, and the number of plaits varies according to choice or to tradition. The word *braiding,* not plaiting, is used in the United States.

PULSE A horse's pulse rate is normally 36 to 40 beats to the minute.

RISEN CLENCH When a clench rises and comes through from a shoe. This must be attended to immediately to prevent injury to the horse. (See CLENCH.)

ROLLER A strap used to hold a rug on a horse. Some rollers have a metal hoop attached to stop the horse becoming cast in his box. (See CAST.)

SIDESADDLE At one time ladies were not expected to ride astride. They rode with both legs on one side of the horse. A sidesaddle has a flat seat with two pommels, one to hook the right leg over, the other to hold the left knee down. Some skilful riders still ride sidesaddle when hunting and in competitions.

SIRE A stallion. The male parent of a foal.

SPLINT A bony growth between the splint bone and the cannon bone on either the fore or hind legs.

STALL An area or compartment for a horse in a stable. For example, a very large stable can be separated into one or more 'stalls'.

STALLION A horse, not under four years, used for breeding. See SIRE.

SUMMER SHEET Usually made from cotton or linen to keep flies from a horse's coat in hot weather.

SWEAT SHEET A form of rug used to keep a horse cool in summer months. This sheet is also used to cover a horse when it is hot.

TACK A word meaning 'saddlery'.

TACK ROOM A place where all tack and equipment is kept.

UNDERFACE When a horse is asked to jump obstacles far too low for its abilities. This can, in most cases, be as wrong as over-facing.

YEARLING A word used for a colt or filly throughout the year after birth.

Index